PO - LI - TIK - N

BLACK REALITY SPOKEN PT 1

Naeriyah JoAn B Daniel Dyer

authorHOUSE®

AuthorHouse™
1663 Liberty Drive
Bloomington, IN 47403
www.authorhouse.com
Phone: 1-800-839-8640

Published by AuthorHouse   10/25/2012

ISBN: 978-1-4772-7898-7 (sc)

Any people depicted in stock imagery provided by Thinkstock are models, and such images are being used for illustrative purposes only.
Certain stock imagery © Thinkstock.

This book is printed on acid-free paper.

the
GALLERY

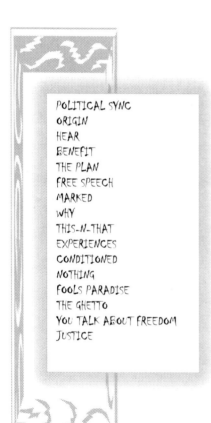

PO - LI - TIK - N

~POLITICAL SYNC~

What do you know about politics?

Probably NOT as much as you think!

Hypocrisy plays a major part in it all this bureaucratic ink

Laws are made while we snooze

Another plan to make us loose

They put it in a book and you don't look..... hidden in pages

Then they say it's our fault because we fail to read the law

And even worst it's an open book for us to look

To seek and find what has been lined while we slept from 9 to 9

Political Sync

That's what being aware of it is

Designed to mask and cover the stink

Most are not aware of the crucial link

That's created in the darkest night life much different than the streets

And the way we think

~ORIGIN~

Very few people know their origin; sad to say I am one of the few

Yet I hunt every day to find my way

Very few people find their origin needless to say I am one of the few

Who has found my way

Very few people seek their origin undisputed truths, lineage hidden paths

Heritage buried or simply erased

But.... I am one of the few whom has uncovered the graves

Opened the tombs, re-trotted the paths, sough the truth regardless of its
mask, stood up and faced the pain, the hurt, the disgrace
that it made that last

I am NOT ashamed of my past

I have reclaimed my lost heritage

I have took back my lineage, my culture, my values, and morals

My Life

I share the truth, the lies, the stories through it all it builds my character, my
strengths, my song, my Right of Passage

I alone spot lights My Origin on a daily basis without a traces

I refuse to loose what I have gained and found and refurbished

I will fight, secure and guard what is rightfully mine.

But, one time

Was stolen from me,

Castrated from my life !

Buried alive.

Choked with a lie,

Drown with silence

In a watery grave,

Disappeared as to never ever been here or born

Now standing affirmed

Rooted, grounded like a rock

Strong like a tree

From its origin in the beginning is me.....

MY ORIGIN ~ One to be Proud of

MY ORIGIN ~ One to Share

MY ORIGIN~ No longer Hidden or Locked up or Lost with despair

MY ORIGIN

Rich

Vibrate and Clear

~HEAR~

Written for an audience with sensitive ears

Written for an audience who hides behind fears

Written for an audience who refuses to hear

Soft words, intimate portraits, sensual lyrics, smooth veneer

Written for an audience who's scared to feel

Written for an audience where

Peers dictate their actions daily appeal

Written for an audience who's segregated in society by hypocrisy who shouts democracy yet stifles free speech and dialect in the streets

A portrayal of words composed to evolve used in poet's mouth far different from what they are

Written for an audience who might be liberated enough to withstand the spoken word that's illustrated and allow it to step inside to create a diversion

Written for an audience who has no fear, not afraid to hear, or change to make a stand right here.

Or

Are you that audience? Who sits silent and waits for someone else to manipulate the system for their own means to escape...

Does my words fall on idle ears? Or on water that will rise and create a flood to move steel

~BENEFIT~

BENEFIT: a way by which you incur something by material gain. Knowledge or what have you

BENEFITTED: something you have received from someone or something

BENEFICIAL: something that does you good or is good for you

BENEFICARY: someone who gains from something or someone

What is the Benefit? Is it Beneficial and are you the Beneficiary of its remnants, contents, services, or productions

Is it worth your time, mind and effort what's the Benefits? Can you tell me?

People destroyed in Katrina's awakening complete devastation no serious rescue missions or concern for their survival because there's

NO BENEFIT !

It's an illumination brought alive by the prophecies many animation the only variance

It's Real

No...... Benefits

Now you tell me what's the Benefit ?

People destroyed alive at sea committed to a watery grave.

Who once crossed those dreadful waters in the belly of the Amistad hell, buried alive at all cost

WHY ?

Cause there was NO Benefit

Tsunami' was an act of nature that took lives as it took back its natural state of the land. It's original habitat.

Those people are the Beneficiary

Those people Benefit

To them it was Beneficial

Who decides who benefits here in this great Northern Land called America is it? A course not I, is it me? think again. It's the man they call the government . It's His Hand that Benefits when destruction Hits.....

911 was a plan that failed to kill enough of the human species yet it did what it was suppose to do unite fear in all of you and all people give an excuse for a cause give a reason for a senseless way...   unexcused

Abuse

There's no

Excuse

NOW YOU TELL ME AFTER ALL OF THIS After mass—Who's the Benefitted

Who's the Beneficiary?

What's was Beneficial?

What was the Benefit?

You do the math......

You count up the cost.....

I guarantee you won't calculate out !

~THE ~PLAN~

We have always heard about the Plan.... But did we understand

We always been told to have a plan in hand..... But man did we understand

We continue to plan because if there's no plan.....we have no stand

SOUNDS DIFFICULT !

Would You Agree ?

When the Boat sailed across the seas from England with its captive free.

The Plan was carried out rid England of its Tyrants and Criminal debris and anyone who refused or didn't adhere to England's rules.

So the Plan was carried out on a boat full of outcast— excommunicated from the culture and land they were born in

Grew up in (thrown out) Banded

never to return to their home land if they do would be executed on site.

The Plan—on a boat, a ship a vessel thrown together a group of people from a variety of backgrounds who sought after a place they could call their own and not be persecuted for what they believed or for what they have done.

The Plan—Criminals, Outlaws, Murders, Thief's, Rapists, Liar's,

Fraudulent motifs, Religious, Political activist chiefs set a sail for a land to defeat. One common goal was to find relief so they landed on a soil occupied by nomads' tribes who they called savages because of their ignorance cap side.

Renamed a land already occupied to call it their own a pilgrim's pride. A land built on lies, criminals mind, religious motif, and political asylum, took what wasn't theirs and made captive the tribes killed them with disease and herded them into reservation camp sit

Then crossed the seas to enslave a nation with cruelty

To force a people to build on a land and incur such strife in life and bewilder another life

The Plan– you still don't understand was to see if the unwanted could survive and they did by any means they applied of what they were accused and tried barred

barred from their culture and life to start a new burden on another life. They succeeded and became mighty by fraud, lies and schemes and today is our successor by any means.

NOW DO YOU UNDERSTAND

The Plan Your Living it in this land brought together by a force we fought, We cried, We refused with Pride

But The Plan

Took Over

and secured this land and when

they saw this nation they enslaved

with cruelty was strong the incorporated another plan to de-

Vise a stronger hand to hold the

Captive free to this land that plan

Has been implemented and still

Strives today.

Look around you'll see how its

weaved you and me!

~FREE SPEECH~

I need a lawyer

I need someone to represent my case

Since 911 our free speech is at stake...

Someone asked me how and why we need to fight to keep that right?

Let me simply rectify my claim

We are not TERRORIST simply because we voice our opinion.

We are NOT TERRORIST because our Professors at school request their students to write an opinionated essay.

We are NOT TERRORIST because we disagree with our Presidency and its government bureaucracy

What the elected officials fail to understand is WE the PEOPLE of this land put them in command and WE the PEOPLE of the U.S.A. can replace every one of them

Yet our free speech is compromised and is about to be abolished, controlled and regulated

If WE don't take a stand

Just like OUR Voting Rights Our Ancestors fought and died for is sitting on the chopping block waiting to be erased just like they did the DARKER hue that America calls RACE and are still doing today. A misrepresentation of a word used inappropriately to denote a nation in this land

Land and it is still being done today. Unless WE stand and hold it place WE no longer will have a voice in this space.

WE just can't see it WE blinders in OUR face....

There's NO excuse for ignorance to the laws it's an open docket available to US ALL. As we sleep a goodnights rest laws are passed and placed into effect while society records this. The ONLY reason the majority is blind and deaf

Because they refuse to read what's in BOLD they haven't been told it's hidden in a book right under their nose a book they won't openly address.
So Now you been enlighten to the overseers..... The Plan is to stay ahead of the game You must obtain the knowledge and keep your rights left in plain view in this land

AND

FREE SPEECH is ONLY One of them!

~MARKED~

What a Fantastic WORD

MARKED

WE ARE MARKED GENERATION

Trying to erase the debilitation

ONLY making a mess of realization.

We have converted to devastation.

Some may ask HOW are we marked? I present to those that

that ask that simple question-

Just LOOK around...........

We mark ourselves by looking down

We mark ourselves by wearing clothing half mass (like the flag goes half mass when an important figure dies-I guess we must be resembling a generation that has died)

We mark ourselves by what we do I we think some

how it's cool .

We mark ourselves by following the entertainment industry never realizing it's all a staged visionary meant to enjoy NOT to employ by following your boi and gurl.

We mark ourselves by the WORDS we use—the terms of endearment we think is tremendous. Never realizing its dimension's is killing us while at the same time demeaning us

We don't think before we talk, walk, or dress trying to impress

What the effect of what we represent.

We rather be marked and stand out and be noticed leaving a bad taste YET that keeps us ALL extremely noted.

~WHY~

Many ask the question WHY we are the way we are?

Many wonder WHY we're born into the families that are parched.

Many question YAH (GOD)

Some question Man

The answers those receive are void of understanding and wisdom.

Many ask the? I ask WHY Do I still cry

ABBAH, they all are gone and still the tears run.

Many ask the? WHY do I hurt the way I do, Only left with unknown reasons, no explanation due

I ask why so many times I'm sure so many of you have too.

When the truth finds its way home it's unacceptable to you.

Many ask when will it STOP or simple just disappear or vanish in thin air out of sight that I

Can't see....

I only sense the facts remain we're a shame, unprepared and don't even want to go there..

WHY YAH - Creation of all living matter:

WHY DO I STILL CRY

WHY DO I STILL HURT

WHY DO I STILL WONDER WHY

Why can't I accept things that I

Know I cannot change.

Why does it matter NOW?

I'm grown

I'm old and almost home

But still I wanna know WHY it is the way it is

Why it had to be this way

WHY??

~THIS-n-THAT~

When you dress like that you represent this

When you dress like this you represent that

Why not be all you can be by presenting your mind and capabilities

When you dress like that it STOPS you y the door

When you dress like this opportunities flow galore

You wonder why you got it so hard

STOP and THINK of your décor what your wearing and displaying

Trying to get on the floor

Your being judged from head to toe before you have a chance to express your core

~EXPERIENCES~

WE ALL CRAVE EXPERIENCES IN SOME FORM, SHAPE OR FASHION

WE CAN IMAGINE, IN VISION, AND FANTASYE EXPERIENCES

SO WE DON'T LISTEN OR HEED THE CAUTION THE WARNINGS

THE FLASHING LIGHTS

ALL FOR THE MOMENT OF

EXPERIENCES

WE TAKE THE FLIGHT

~CONDITIONED~

Take a moment to reflect on life itself, step back in time and realize this concept, as a people we been conditioned to accept what society deems right

We refuse to acknowledge the light as generations rise and pass that we created a population designed to self-destruct.

We been conditioned I don't want you to forget this word "CONDITIONED" is the reason

We react, respond, re-live, reproduce, retrace, retract, restart, retention, retain, regain, re-examine, re, re, re, re, re, re.

We need to STOP and LOOK at our surrounding venue. We as a people need to STOP and CHECK our lives, the way we live, what we believe, what we do, what we say, what we value, what we expect, how we treat one another and their possessions.

We need to REALIZE we have manufactured a culture, a people, a society and generations that disrespects, manipulates, takes advantage of any and all situations, greedy, materialistic, selfish, vulgar, ruined, no manners, no values, no morals, no standards, Just lies, steals, cheats, destroys, kills sounds like O'Lucifer, HaSatan, the Devil, the Prince of this world, the Prince of lights, the Prince of peace, your GOD, your Master whom you serve without thought or relief in delight You've been conditioned

and never realized your defeat

We are like pods planted in a garden manufactured by themselves, duplicated like clones, no resilience just assistance to a society we call a democracy. We call free and brave, full of opportunities that are hypocritic, suicidetic, mentally cradled, blinded, deaf, partially mute and crippled by their own hand in the stoop.

When will YOU realize you been

conditioned let's bring it to reality something you can speculate

maybe even relate if possible too. In our neck of the woods, North Continent we call America built on lies, deception, dishonesty, thieves, murders, those of self-destruction; those of ill minds and abuse intended to die in the seas and the oceans of this world by those Kings and Queens who ostracized, banned, banished, excommunicated them from the United Kingdom,

Europe's lawless clan that's who built AMERICA !

So they could create havoc on another people for their sins their land they stand alone with those whose plight for religious freedom the so called Pilgrims landed on the soil of the Native Americans aka Armenians and committed acts of treason for which they need not worry about being reprimanded for their assaults, sins and ill will to mankind

goes unpunished for their guilty obstructive ways by a law

they created to hide themselves from justice being served on them. They are so guarded by their own laws to prevent others for committing the same or like manner of atrocities being used or done on them.

CONDITIONED you must come to realize you are CONDITIONED

No matter your hue; No matter how you came to be on this Northern pew WE call soil

Your Conditioned, washed, a fixated by a man made society govern by the lawless who call themselves politicians, judges, law keepers , The House of Representatives– who they representing certainly not US, Congress, Senators, Mayors with their money and possessions they do block and lock you OUT

So you won't achieve their level of glory and fame the right to survive in a land they made.

It's an illusion for you and me to strive till we die; a dream to become what we will never accomplish.

To prepare and plan for their off-springs future not ours; to fulfill and promote this land and create a society for all of them

No, NO, fingers are being pointed this is just a wakeup call to get you acquainted with what's about to fall

You've Been Conditioned

WAKE UP YA"LL

WAKE UP

~NOTHING~

Look in my eyes what do you see? Nothing, Nothing, Nothing

You see baby I'm in this world too facing reality... trying to live and be free.

Tomorrows dreams may bring sorrow, happiness and even pain.

We call this the pit stop—between Satan's role and the LORD's Almighty call And I still

See Nothing, Nothing, Nothing

My oh my, what a day a fool can

spring living and dying so it may seem; Although happiness is the highest plea and cry; the sadness seems to still be!

My heart aches with loneliness

My mind at a distance

My soul in a Hole

My consciousness at a breaking point

And me,

I'm still starving and dying from thirst and the man calls this equality, motivation, living, growing constantly in reality!

And . . .

I'll Just be DAMN

I still see

Nothing

NOTHING

NOTHING!

~FOOL'S PARADISE~

You live and you die

In a fool's paradise

And

Your accomplishments

don't mean a thang

You lay awake and

You finally realize

That you're here bound

And

Chained

I said your living now

In a fool's paradise

And

The man is playing his childish games. You take away the lite and on comes
the nite

BOOM !

LOOK OUT !

Here comes the Pain

Oh baby, how does it feel to be living here? Where fantasy envy's reality? !

Say Brother, your living now in a fool's paradise and whitey gots Superfly tamed living now

In a fool's paradise

Money and Fame won't help the

Flame

The white man got us trapped here in his fingers of hell while he twiddles his thumbs of little games

~THE GHETTO~

The ghetto black

The ghetto white

Tell me my people why do we fight/

We fight to be free, but

Sometimes in the struggle of fighting a battle for peace

We get tired, frustrated, defeated, depressed and lose

AND ~ we're suppose to be cool like fools ! (ha,ha,ha)

Tell me my people's color a barrier?

For I wear no false face, personality or smile

Listen my brotha's and Sista's

My appearance is what you see

And

As I hear it, is what you get

And

Believe me it's definitely what

I got

Not even death could tear it apart

PO~

LI~

TIK~

N

~YOU TALK ABOUT FREEDOM~

You talk about freedom

You talk about peace and happiness

You talk about love and warmth

But, nobody talks about hate and sadness

You talk about the friendship train

You talk about life itself

You talk about having your way

But, never think about death!

Let me tell you something people and listen to me good because what is coming down we must say we understood.

Understanding is a groovy point and put a little trust cause that's a must and quit trying each other my brother for there's little to gain by yourself.

As for my black sister, dig my game you also put a little understanding with a little more trust and stand by your brother whether or not he be your man

Because that's a must....

YES stand my sister at your man's side sometimes it won't hurt.

Now if you can talk about anything

Talk about Revolution

Talk about the future and present

Talk about NOW

Never the past is forgotten just pushed to the subconscious side

Always the future awakes us which lye's ahead. Think and act on life itself. The stage is set we must Do It Ourselves.

You must remember that !

Our mother is a black woman

Our father is a black man

Our sisters and brothers are black; we must fight to protect ourselves.

YOU! If your to talk about anything be hip to what you know and if you don't know—get

hipped. Progress with vitality and priority strive with confidence and strong self-determination.

In other words live my People

For what you were.; For what you are And For what you may become

And then you can begin to talk

about freedom, peace and happiness, love and warmth because there is no hate or sadness in our world. Believe in taught in ourselves

What we know is what we realize

What is the truth and what lye's ahead

Forget the society which is today surround yourself beauty

Talk about freedom

Talk about love

Talk about peace and happiness

Talk about warmth and freedom

Talk about Togetherness and what has been

~JUSTICE~

2 wrongs don't make it right

Three justice systems

Each with their own set of laws and consequences

Don't make it equal

Each portraying its own set of rules

No you have not realized how

JUST-ICE

Mandated doing what's right

How it became job security

and

law-yers who mostly are liars for an

astronomical $price$....

are as bad as some Doctors

who went to school

who went to school to have physicians' rights to practice and experiment on people's lives

to proclaim genocide on a people who came to trust their insight to prescribe for their living rights yet instead became their test sites

human genny pigs , worse than Rats and monkeys that bite

serve you right! When will America see the light?

People stand up and fight

Fight America for what's RIGHT

NOT JUSTICE – Just-Ice –Freezing

Over each parasite and documenting the wrongs and the rights this is heresy
at its best in flight

Out to get ALL who are not on the same plight.

Just-

ICE

That's how cool it is!

~LAWS~

While you sleep

We negotiate

Wake up half white

Slept naked thru the night

Now you ain't right

LAWS are CLAWS

That litigate

Multiply

To facilitate

Transgression

A diplomatic mess

Meditate

Translate

Demonstrate

Got up late

Forsake your mate

Prescribe date

To fornicate

   All disguised in a LAW that makes you want to regurgitate

                    LaWs

          LAWS

                    LawS

             THAT'S ALL FOLKS

If you would've been woke you would had felt the choke...

~HAIKU"S~

I ask Questions

I get NO answers

So I continue

Making sense of things

Understanding things

Realizing things

Complicated things aren't a must!

Simple statements

Fake & True

Remind me of words

Recited by you

Use

My Right to Vote

Take a note

A smoted joke

The end of a PLAN

No man understands

IF

He did he respect me

Repent & live Righteously

Money don't change you so the story goes that's what I been told

Money will conform you if enough is at your door

Sometimes money causes envy, greed and strife with stress if its right

Especially if your needs succeeds

It doesn't matter that you get a little piece

What matters is that it's expected you share till your bare...

Money left or given in death to a soul is incomparable and only free to use it when they are totally alone the only beneficiary

Sister's & brothers & children find a need to great the need so they all can escape leaving you as you were in the beginning with pennies to relate

It doesn't matter if you give –you never give enough. So it's better not to give and bare the hatred from them both

Cause no one is truly satisfied and they find ways to nullify an aggression and definition to personify the need for help

What would they have done if there wasn't none $ $ $

Continue on their journey that they begun

Strange how money creates a need for some

It banishes the wish list and makes you the source list

For reality alone

I'd rather be poor but that does one no good cause they still expect you to share your crumps in despair

I guess it's called misery who loves company and his cousins who drop in but, that's another poem to sew and read in

Not today cause it's ALL about the $ $ $

You got some to share because I sure need some my pockets are about bare

~WHERE DID WE GO WRONG~

Where did we go wrong

The list today is practically endlessly long

Let's start with the simple things in life

Best described as religion coupled with politics

Mixed with opinionated beliefs

Regardless the system is dramatically wrong

A Thought

"It is said that history repeats itself"

When I first started college in Colorado

I heard these same explicit words

Instantly a debate; my argument..... HOW CAN AYONE BE SO STUPID? If it didn't work previously then in the past.....WHY would you think it would work now?

Especially in 2011 going into 2012

Now the clique, "WHY RENVENT THE WHEEL? IF IT'S NOT BROKE DON'T FIX IT! IF IT DON'T WORK REVAMP IT!

Enough is enough is ENOUGH !!!!!!!

MEN who think & believe that he knows how to fix the ailments of this world just digged the graves a little deeper for the generations to come

WARNING this book is gonna jump ALL over the place

Sometimes you might find it a blessing or not especially if it forms a chronological order that is fitting to follow

Let's make one correction PLEASE in the words we use because people love talking words out of its true content and using it as a definition for something else then what it's meant for: Oh Well... what I am talking about let me explain...

#1 WORD = RACE

Does NOT, will NOT ever depict a people of any specification

We have so many words that can and will depict a people "RACE" is NOT one of them. It's one of those sound good words; try using nationality, human-beings, and humans

Just like President Obama is not the 1st Black President-YET he is the first Black President to be acknowledged openly & globally in regards to his hue.......... isn't that amazing!

The first wrong doing was the landing of the pilgrim settlers, the Columbus dude who didn't discover America....

You take a Native of their land and displace and dispose of them in a way that is unethical, steal their land, make them an outsider/prisoner on their own soil then charge them to live on it where it once was free and shared economically...

If that isn't LUDICRIS! What is?

TODAY WE TRY........................

Political candidates are very tackless instead of tasteful

Political campaigns are critical antidotes instead of

Instead of critizing the President for a mess he did not create

Why not try helping your President clean up the past administrations desecrations because talk is cheap

make an impression

action speaks louder than words

IF you have a plan that will work

why not use it now instead of waiting to get to the big O

You may not realize you have more power now to change things

Before you reach your final destination the White House,,,,

~MIXER~

Everybody's got a mix

Like the drink @ a bar

Mixer's delight, America's fright

Nothing but, a mixer up mix

That deflects this countries light

~S – T – R – U – G – G – L – E~

Struggle is something we all do at one time or another

Not many people consider it a struggle

To conform or abide, be obedient to survive

Not many people struggle

Like me   but I have

Not many people fight for what is right

Like me   but I do

Not many people speak their mind

Like me   but I can

Not many people stand

Like me   but I remain

Not many people have a voice

Like me   but I sound off

Not many people are courageous

Like me   but I am

Struggle is our middle name

That's all we know in this political land of games

~VOTE~

So Much Commotion To

Do Such A Little Thing

Candidates Dehumanize

Their Competitions Fate

Where is The Morals, Values, and Standards

And Righteousness They State

What Happen To The Dignity And Character

They Make Claims And Mark Their Slates With Promises

To Do This And That

And We Listen To The Hype And Comply

We Entertain And Believe All The Crap

That The Runners place In Our Face

Truly They Have Our Interest On Their Plates

Our Fate Is At Stake

Once In Office They Share No Face

They Got what They Wanted From Us

The Primary Final Vote

Our Mistake

~POLITICALITY~

I sat at the table of democracy and filled my plate with hyprocracy's

Seasoned with immortality, I drank a cup of apathy,

Idle with activity I asked a friend

to sit with me at the table of democracy.

He said he could plainly see I was situated with stupidity and called my food sublimity when it grew from the seed iniquity

Insulted by his brevity, I answered him with levity and asked of what society he ate!

~CONVERSATION PIECE~

I was

Attempting the advocate

noting the diplomat

Who said

Obviously the system sat

In front of the procrastinate

So

Immediately he spat

belligerently

In grouse appearance said

            REPENT!

For WHAT ?

the idiot replied

It wasn't I

Who spat or sat

Nor

Said Repent for that!

Not I   That I am

~LIBERTY~

Liberty and freedom turned inside out

No earthly meaning: ONLY telling us lies and inserting doubt

Freedom is worthless until the truth has set you free

Violence is a distorted mind left

with no peace in time

A society gone wild

An act of greed, where money buys you authority

Knowledge is the key that will

But will my freedom and liberty become a reality?

~RIGHTEOUSNESS~

We are a people with

A right to vote

A right to free will

A right to free speech

A right to become our dream

We are a people whose been

Denied all our life

The right to love

The right to choose

The right to stand

The right to freely walk as a human

As we believe

We are a people who have persevered all our life

Thru the storm

Thru the rain

Thru the fire

Thru the flood

Thru the day we were born

We are a people WHO have

Overcome

With

Righteousness

By doing what is right

Against ALL odds

~PO*LIC~TIK.N~

A sinners delight..... A sinners date..... tic toc mate

Till it STOPS on the dot

Po........ is...... Poor..... the Po Po next door

Tic .... Toc..... like a clock ......magic spot

Campaigners date all the states

Making claims and promises to get in the gate

They get lost once they slivered into the Oval Office

The trauma continues with the drama as another seats in

They take their finances & yours too

Some have millions & school you

From state to state like a bee they pollenate every being into
training doing what it takes to line the pockets of a gamblers
estate making claims and promises so the people will fall in place
with their minds create an avalanche debate
Po li tik n a talented scheme politicians make

Taste the drama
       Wasted dolla

          Time is frayed
Whiles the lies get mandated, sugar coated, marinated, often gets
contaminated to fuck up the American dream they hate
 while everyone enjoys this expensive charismatic plate

~The last HAIKU 4 U~

Live

Laugh

Love

Believe

Righteousness

Faith.......

~AMERICA~

America the beautiful

No more you lost your beauty

America land of the free

Barely you can see

America the prosperity has burned

America has triggered a society that's turned.

America can you regain your dignity

America the land of dreams for refugees

America how can you stand

America you have lost your pride

America can you survive

Beyond the hopelessness you have fathered / mothered

America have you forgotten how you were born?

Where you came from?

How you were formed?

America look at you NOW

Look at your waste

Look at your momentum

Look at your future

America you have lost your morals and morale to greed

America you have gave up your spirit to materialism need

America you have lost your composure

America, America, morbid America

No More America

America has died

~SPANGLED BANNER~

I pledge alliance to a flag of the United States of America unto
the Republic for which it stands
One nation under God, Indivisible with Liberty and Justice for
All
America the beautiful has lost her beauty yeah

America land of the free has bondage all that enter thee

America, America
Why are you blind with greed

America deaf to violence

No self-esteem buried all morality

America has lost her touch; has grown wild with her lust

America who once stood for God

Has been brain washed into memory yeah you know that job

I pledge alliance to a flag that promises me no freedom in the
United States of America unto the Republic for which I stand
striped of my dignity; one nation

under God where the homeless

are left dying in the streets .

A people who idolizes materialism and greed; with no liberty and
no justice yet for some instead of for All where the children gun
down the law

I pledge allegiance to the flag of that sheds no blood of the

United States of America where life has drowned in flooded
spaces

unto the Republic for which it stands leaves no woman, or man
or child alive

One nation under God without dignity and pride indivisible with liberty

and injustice for ALL that are not deployed or left dying and cold in

this hole and wall.

~-~-SCOUNDREL-~-~

A myth if you don't believe

A sly schemish spirit

that flows desperately to deceive

A beautiful gem he once was

Created out of imagery

An illuminating voice rang throughout the clouded sky

With a booming sound can you

Imagine such a skillful soul seeking whom he may devour, steal, kill, and destroy your dreams,

Words and secrets if you reveal

He has names by many which are known

Beware of his disguises for he'll tempt you into his homeless state of mind.

Prepare you for his bewildered wickedness Loudly laughing at you, leaving you clearly naked, undressed, and petrified at the seams

~TREND X~

What will they come up with next........

A Trend that cast a style that last only a little while

TREND X

Colors, remember when we didn't have to think about that.... We could wear any color that caught our eye until TREND X came along and banded it by branding it: the RED for the bloods, the BLUE for the cripts, BROWN for the Hispanic sects. Rainbow for the gays

While others use symbols to recognize their demise to their domains; Not realizing it's all just a game.

At times it's the side of the tracks they try'n to take back; to which side of the streets you can walk onto the block you live on. TREND X is a dilemma born out of poverty unveiled in society created out of liberation for sustentation. What an obliteration people have illustrated in this nation.

TREND X

has you wearing styles thinking it's cool, full of bling, bling , creeping, smoking, doing all kinds of dopin - killin, stealin, claimin - while riding on a dime bewildering in size s each day goes by..... You think you livin the life HIGH IN STYLE WILD wasting away all the while.

TREND X

got all and I did say ALL our black men blinded by the Glitter
and Glow of money, gold, silver, diamonds, SUVs, Mercedes
Benz, hoopdy rims, cars that rock, sounds that block all that
kinda stupid crock. If I had to give a resemblance it would be like
cock blocking stopping someone else from coppin getting the
girl or the boi or job or anything at all.

TREND X

has men in zuit suits wearing their pants on their thighs half
mass couldn't run if they needed to save their lives passing.
shown the bootie and all their draws not realizing their giving a
bootie call to the closest mob; then they get mad and wanna
busta cap cause they get a hit from displaying the pit....it's their
fault should've pulled and kept them up them pants that's
dragging and grabbing your thighs embracing your knees your
disgracing your family and especially me. Even got some
women, girls and females thinking its hip to dress and display
their hips... when you get raped you can't escape the distasteful
temptation you gave.

 OOOH but it's just a Trend it will end, it will pass, it won't last yet
it comes again

TREND X won't STOP unless WE open our eyes, ears, and mind
and become wise and understand what it's doing to our kind!

~1/4 ERASED ~

Erased...1/4th of the Human Species we call a RACE...Is *it* YOU?

1/4th of the population
is being erased,
extinguished , depleted,
and as crazy as it
seems just simply
deleted. AND they
don't even know it or
realize their estate is
vanishing. Where are

they going? Maybe you can tell me; of course I have a good idea
it's called GENOCIDE!!! by popular demand.

 Today's cultures are so diversified especially here in America;
and ONLY in America can you find such outrageous diversity
with no real back bone to define its simplicity, cultural heritage,
lineage, or ancestral line. Those born here can't link to their own
there's none. Have it your way; do it your style; ONLY in America
can you live life wild, manmade trends in a society that grins with
no teeth. People come from all over to live in America; Land of
prosperity, the place to be... Yet 1/4th of the

Human species we call a race is being ERASED in droves. You
say how and why could this be? Look at your people those
who've struggled for centuries to accomplish a dream forgotten

in the main stream, buried alive on borrowed time. Look at the image generations beyond our ancestors are portraying; Look at where we are today, physically, mentally, financially, spiritually, from yesterday and where we'll be tomorrow from today.

 In actuality we haven't gone very far; yet the illusions of appearance visualize a delusion. We have progressed a mile stone further than our ancestors ever expected us to go; Yet they had hopes, ambitions, dreams, that they scoped. Yet our men are dying in a fashion inscribed and documented in time. BUT we as a people do nothing to commit our minds and fall in line. Our men die in prison locked up beyond time, they die on the streets trying to make a dime, and they die at the hand of

 their own with defeat, and they take their own lives and cap their fellow man in the streets. They defile their bodies with drugs, alcohol, violence and guns claiming a territory that's not even their own. A color, a code, killing each other by their own hands and doing it alone that's benefitting the man! Someone please tell me PLEASE when will this end? By the trends they keep, the styles they immolate, the speech they perpetrate trying to be King with no throne or domain of their own.

Our women have taken great lengths of their own to the point of degrading themselves with no crown; trying to fit in and get even at any stake. They've accomplished great goals; their dreams they behold; their powerful BUT at what price have they sacrificed their royal role as a Queen on their throne?

We as a people are being erased by society with great grace and

pace and political mace and greed beyond materialism need has
pacified our

gates. Replaced our culture with someone else's fate; We've
traded our inheritance away for disgrace.
What's sad about it we don't even realize our state. The 1/4th of
the human species we call a race is being erased..... Is it YOU?

~'BORN POSSIBILE'~

Born in a land of possibilities

Given a chance to succeed as you please where everyone
originates from sea to sea

Once called a melting pot full of

Diversity and plots

{do realize it's all a game you are the organized pieces fitting
into a puzzle realm}

In reality the faces are like chess

Which one fits you best

{wait, wait one minute oooooh that's too long..... Cause in

America it plays by seconds}

There's no particular culture to

Invest everyone dresses to impress

Someone called it keeping up with the Jones; I call it dabbling

In a bed of Roses with thorns in the mist. Everyone's business is
no bodies business.

The plan was to create One kind, One culture, One standard

One way, One mind. Unfortunately No One figured The Plan

'would fold, turn out the way it

did. BUT IT DID !!!

You know why?

~UNFORSEEN JOURNEY~

Born in a world that's diseased

Forced to be raised you don't wanna be. Placed in a radical society defending the righteous way you believe. No one ever knows exactly how you feel. When you try to express from your heart what's real. People have a bad case of comprehending syndrome of what's being said it's like a virus that's being spread throughout your system

Sometimes it takes you out

Sometimes you carry it about

Whatever the reason for its existence it's killing Black Folks for sure without a doubt. It's invaded my body for years from head to toe it's been eating at the insides tearing it up as it goes till it appears on the outside and the whole world knows. The appearance is downright disgusting and ugly but, I have it too? Trying to find a cure before

It ceases me too. The symptoms are sadness, loneliness for sure can be downright depressing and painful too. The hurt alone leaves tracks everywhere just like a user who uses needles to take him somewhere else.

It's an unforeseen journey I'm telling you. Its causes division in an unknown lane when you're fighting not to be divided but, you

can't even stand. You long for closeness but, it's no where
In sight. You fight hard to heal all the devastation you got inside
but, no matter how long you struggle to be free or how good the
fight the battle rages on with no end in sight. Over and Over you
ask forgiveness for this plight. You try to forget it but, it pops
back insight. You try to be the best person you can be, you try to
do right with each person you see, or victim that reaches or help,
you too face the reality.

It's a never ending destruction till everyone's dead. What's left is
the seed to carry on the thread which quickly develops into a
rope made to choke you up with the past that last and last you
run away fast that does you no good. That's another journey
that's misunderstood.

We try so hard not to cry the tears of release deep down inside.
We try to understand why

The persecution rides. We so far from the truth that will set us
free all we do is hide. Not wanting to accept our part and
responsibility. Every time an incident occurs , it resurfaces each
time getting harder and harder to overcome and ask for
forgiveness that doubles genetically especially when you have
not done nothing wrong and got nothing to hide or you
previously already asked for forgiveness a trillion times. Never
the less I am forced to perform the chant

 It's a never ending destruction till everyone's dead. What's left is
the seed to carry on the thread which quickly develops into a

rope made to choke you up with the past that last and last you run away fast that does you no good. That's another journey that's misunderstood.

We try so hard not to cry the tears of release deep down inside. We try to understand why

from the truth that will set us free all we do is hide. Not wanting to accept our part and responsibility. Every time an incident occurs , it resurfaces each time getting harder and harder to overcome and ask for forgiveness that doubles genetically especially when you have not done nothing wrong and got nothing to hide or you previously already asked for forgiveness a trillion times. Never the less I am forced to perform the chant

of forgive me over and over again a never ending state that drives me insane.

An unforeseen journey constantly traveling at times you get tired and frustrated of the constant bickering that chipes, keeps you moving around an about telling your story inside out. You wonder will this journey ever end cause at that moment that flash it seems like it just the beginning. A never ending story designed like a saga

With continuous scenes of lives performed with a magnitude so greatly created the occasion to slide into a illusional state of mind.

This Unforeseen Journey will forever be in a phase. Accountability is what's needed within a spoiled mi

~CORRECT THE SYSTEM~

Today we live in a corrupt society where our government tries to correct the third world countries system while letting their own fall to the wayside.

Today our court system is out of bounds. Instead of innocent until proven guilty IT'S NOW GUILTY UNTIL PROVEN INNOCENT!!!

If you have enough money to prove the system wrong = the police arresting documents, the prosecuting attorney's competition to WIN a case instead of TRUTH and the judge who is the deciding scale of justice to uphold the evidence as crucial or bogus findings comes down to choice who side is the judge on ?

Whose side will the judge choose truth or lies to keep the peace the choice will always be in most cases the system in place..... That wins the case and the victim is at stake and confined till they find someone to plead their innocence and prove injustice has over looked and mistaken truth for the lies the officers of the law and the prosecuting attorney sworn before the judge and citizens to be true.

NOW those are the lies that have ruined a LIFE for life! That ain't right where's the justice in that? WHO then will CORRECT the SYSTEM that has crucified a life. All has taken an oath to serve

And have traded it in for $$$$ MUCH MULAH instead of TRUTH

that sets you free. Lawyers have become Liars and thieves which are a change of venue that is backwards in a system that is suppose to be righteous in its plight.

Today our Attorneys who taken in by so called white collar crime.

Victims of the system that serve unjust sentences, a loss of time and unproductive life because they cannot afford to pay for their freedom to prove their

innocence are forced to take a plea deal that puts them behind

bars sometimes for most of their life; they spend their time in confinement trying to find the proof to set them free from a different worldly environment they are sentenced to be in.

While our law officers who are sworn to protect and serve the

 community and its citizens the majority rather lie, cheat, steal, exploit, profile groups of diversity then to seek the truth find the real cause and persecute the right individuals. What's even worst and more profound is those who have paid their debt to society and finished their prison time, served their probation ARE still being persecuted by the quote on quote free society as criminals with no second chance to prove they community and its citizens the majority rather lie, cheat, steal, exploit, profile groups of diversity then to seek the truth find the real cause and persecute the right individuals. What's even worst and more profound is those who have paid their debt to society and finished their prison time, served their probation ARE still being persecuted by the quote on quote free society as criminals with no second chance to prove they have changed.

The judicial system brands you with many types of tags some deserving some not so deserving however it never changes it just strengthens their plight against mankind especially those of one kind. We see this all the time.... Felonies are a strong hold to keep a man down sometimes its legit but, most of the time it's unwarranted.

The judicial system is just as soiled as it was 4,000 years ago and as it is said history repeat itself a truth most of us fret. We just haven't got it, we have not learned it, and WE just DON'T see it or RECOGNIZE it ....YET!!!!!

Those who head the judicial system are followers of another system that only believes in its own justified beliefs that have come to rest as a system in distress but no one wants to protest so they just let it rest ......what a MESS!

~INFLAMED JUSTICE~

Have you as an individual ever felt inflammation in your extremities? If you have not then you have no idea how painful it is or can be. It is an muscle or ligament that has become injured and is now inflamed, swollen, hot to the touch and makes you immobile unable to move freely from place to place which becomes extremely difficult to maneuver and get around . I have just described to you

Inflamed justice in this society at its best

The mess that society created to test the replacement for entrapment another source for enslavement; that would be justified inside the walls of the law and discrimination cannot touch this criminal illegal entrapment composed of laws that are unjustified but solidified by an inflamed justice where we ALL abide and reside

 insanely inside on a crucified lie.

How remotely subtle has America become yet it's very identifiable to which it has grown from.

Inflamed Justice is only a portion of the government that is far from the norm.

~the JUDGE~

The judge...... whose the judge?

The judge who judges YOU

Who judges the judge? That judged you?

Good Question ....??? good question

But is there an answer?   of course there is.......

IT IS WRITTEN in the SCRIPTURES from the beginning of time

Recorded in Matthew 7:12

TO BE RIGHTEOUS; NOT UNRIGHTEOUS simply means doing what is right

against what is not right = wrong.... however our judges have it twisted in

nature and by law infringed in fear they weigh un-righteously against the

righteous causing undue judgment

~ECONOMICAL GARBAGE~

Once upon a time in a land just like ours.....

Taxes were confined to a particular commodity like luxury and cars and homes and not a reoccurring entity.

Today should be like yesterday once you buy a home you own it and it's yours NOT taxed yearly for something already purchased and fully paid for in its entirety.

Economical garbage I say.........

Another way to keep a hold on your belongings is to keep taxing you after you paid.

Another way to use your tax dollar up is to build prisons for men, woman, and juveniles and then lie and say it helps the economy, creates jobs......job security that is!

When in reality it supports the very enemy that's stares you in the face day to day

Economical garbage I say.........

A thirty year Mortgage on a 3 bedroom home that costs you a whopping 75,000 in a poor neighborhood by the time you're done paying you have put out of pocket 150,000 with all the taxes you have paid over the thirty year loan when the deed says you own it there should not be any more taxes on the land or the home you now own. Once you pay thirty thousand for a new A new car and 72 months to pay It off which happens to be something like 6 years there's taxes included in that which if calculated right you have just brought a house on wheels because you just finish paying close to 60,000 or more for a car that supposedly cost thirty

Thousand when you first signed those papers.

Economical garbage I say

The taxes we pay are beyond

reason per say. The government is chosen by the people and it is the people who should govern the government to cut down on white collar crime and blue collar crime alike. Our economical growth has caused us to go blind where logic should have stepped in.

Once upon a time we own land we could pass down to our children's, children or will to a relative and keep it in the family

That is rarely seen anymore or even available to do today. Our tags for our cars especially if the car is brand spanking new cost as much as a car note to register and receive a thumb print of a tag that can be peeled in a minute.

Economical garbage I say......

Let the political government from top to bottom get a job instead of being sanctioned with pay, homes, cars, vacation subsidies, free planes and the like.

Economical garbage I say......

When you're done serving a political office you still get compensated with a nice lot of funds to continue living on in a manner in which you were accustomed to........BS

Economical garbage I say.....

If anyone should be compensated for their time served is the military personnel for they gave their life to defend a country that is not just or righteous

When our military personnel return home they are jobless, unemployed and possibly homeless and all they may have received is a salute and a honorary mental as a sign of achievement but no honor is recognized when you cannot live, breathe and survive in a land you gave your life for to defend, protect and honor for life. You're just another soldier driven home after war might as well be another white tombstone

 In the grave yard cemetery

Economical garbage I say.......

We have homeless people because it political savvy it gives the politicians something to do when they are not crushing each other on the senate floor.

Economical garbage, I say....

America's debt is not the fault of its people..... It is the fault of its Political Core we call Government. Take away their lavish spending and put the work in Martha's Vineyard and America could be out of debt before you know it.

Economical Garbage I say....

Take away the unnecessary prisons that house nonviolent criminals then they will have room enough for the violent if they would use their pea brains to think America could be #1 again. Stop lending to every country in need help them yes to succeed but keep your bank

Out of their hands. That's one way to gain back the economic plan. Reach out if you must using other resources and such but the dollar bill should have never been jeopardized and scrutinized as meaningless.

Economical Garbage I say......

How many politicians would campaign for the job if it had no mullah attached to its positions what would you bet there would be multiple openings begging for anyone willing to fulfill the bill.

Economical Garbage I say.....

Our economy is at its pit fall because politicians want it that way, they ride alongside those who play chess in the board rooms nest as a secret hideaway they gamble us away.

What a Political Economical

MESS.....................

Too much to clean up anyway besides all them BSers will do is provide more

clutter in your way. And we don't get PAID!!!!

ECoNOMiCAL GARBAGE

~The BIRTHING of AMERICA~

Does anyone ever stop and think how America became America and turned out this way? The world wasn't named America before the settlers found their way by pilgrimaging on a boat designed for their demise a float. Yet when the tale is told his—story always notes that it was discovered on their way to a new land to betray its host.

Let the truth be told STOP the over casting molds.

America was built on lies and thieves and killers breeze, murders loafs, rapist and bestiality toads and religious propagandist noose. Those who have been exiled as well as excommunicated from their own land born and guided, religious asylum posed as freedom riders.

LOOK at it now and let your conscious be your guidance.

These traitors and prisoners were out casted from their home land set out to sea to die but, fell across a new land fully occupied by natives in this southern region across the water gateway from their distant home land. The outcaste took their land made the natives captives and prisoners in their own home. Now they go about gaining notoriety by conquering others they come to be the greatest in the world. YET they have never went back to claim their own the land they were born in, grew up in and was raised in. unattended as no man's land.

The sad edition to this poem is that they have created a saga that is plaguing their plan. They went to other countries taken their peoples made them their slaves and servants for days and then walk around like that's a normal life and wage..... Let's trade places and see how it pays. I guarantee you would not engage in the play or enjoy the games you used on us as entertainment.

One day people as young as two will learn the truth of the ancestors' fluke.

One day people will tell the truth because it sets them free instead of lying about you and me.

One day this nation will heal and

begin to grow again.

One day we will learn that history ONLY repeats itself when people think what they are doing is different from what's already

been done, redone, and done over AGAIN.

One day we as a people will look at the making of America and realize it was a making of a diabolical dilemma of an insane mind.

One day we will learn that knowledge is POWER, Diversity is POWER and UNITY is POWER wrapped into ONE the GREAT I AM YHWH

One day we will look at our history and realize this did not work

Try something different than divide and conquer and defeat.

One day we will learn that different cultures teaches RESPECT and SELF-RESPECT and to LOVE one another

ONE DAY if we manage not to self-destruct and come to our

senses that 5 greedy men can't monopolize the entire EARTH without ciaos. That their greed could free the World if they would only share their wealth

There would be no need for the occult which only means hidden.

The prosperity would flourish and time will stand still.

America would be beautiful again and will have found her glory but that's not how the story ends.

It's written those greedy men and their generations will never bend.

So America is doomed is the plan. AMEN

~POLITICAL WOES~

Presidential Speeches are just like leeches they drain the blood
from your veins and leave you depending on them

To keep their promises proclaimed in the campaign speeches
used to persuade the masses of people to their side

It's unfortunate the people who make up the democracy do not
uphold their right of free speech soon to be abolished.
Unkept Promises are a defeat, when you tell lies in da street......

Campaign foes

Commodities woes

All a joke for the poo' folk

Political standoffs to defeat your opponent while bad mouthing
each other like comedians do to combat laughter inside the
practical plight to fight what is forgotten is the intelligent
character and charismatic finish associated with dignity,
mannerisms, class, morals that accompany ones stature that
there is no need to stoop low or walk in the path of shallow
waters to present your side of persuasive goals
Riches and Greed have no need

No care to spare for the less fortunate

Until the season to be generous stares

If what you say has any merit.....Do it NOW

If what you say be the truth WHY wait till later for da proof

Don't need stamina or a prestige's title to make a difference or a
change; correct the problem or the issue at hand
Why make PROMISES? Why make STATEMENTS to get you into
office for that occasion you're just a figure head without a voice
ruled by Congress and the DEAD; ruled by the Senate that we
dread; All are states of HEAD...
All the orders recorded in "ROBERTS RULES" that's been
mandated by the fools before YOU...
So when you're President you're the puppet on a string; you will
do most anything... ONLY a voice when they pull your string all
you got is a red button for emergency to ring if we go to war that
won't and don't need approval to pass the gas...... AND...won't
cure a thang!
It's counted as political woes that Americans accumulated
through time and recorded as HIS-STORY in your books to read
as we do through decades passed

KENNEDY

JOHNSON

NIXON

REGAN

BUSH

CARTER

BUSH

CLINTON

And now you trash OBAMA what a gasp for this political mask

of

woes

~RULINGS~

Imprisonment is synonymist to enslavement as it is to
confinement only camouflaged by hues diversified to
make it equal across the lines but, as a collective view
not justified for in captivity you will find all kinds of
crimes against humanity and its kind

Murders

Rapist

Killers

Robbers

Molesters

Thieves

State infractions

Federal indictments

Government implications

Does the time fit the crime and the fine? Are the judges
wasting the tax payers' dime for job security on any line?

Do we really need more jails and prisons to create more
jobs for those who really only want a pay check and
abuse the system by retaliation on the inmate less

fortunate release date so they hate and take out their aggressions misuse and abuse, harassment on those who are in their control.

You ought to do as the Written Word says you know that book you call the Bible

There is a mandate for how to live and survive and handle the crime It's no more harsh then what you have imposed today. Rulings

~BE CAREFUL WHAT YOU SPEAK~

DEATH AND LIFE IS IN THE TONGUE

You know that raw piece of muscle that is meat between your teeth that bleeds when bitten.....

SINCERITY, RIGHTEOUSNESS, BELIEF AND FAITH

All of these things we say and speak and walk but not ALL practice what they preach

How Sincere are you?

Your heart

Your mind

Your soul

All are One

OR

Is what you speak just a BIG whole you know an empty space in place? Holds No Gold or Goal

How Righteous are you?

Your walk

Your talk

Your ways

Your thoughts

Is it reliable, consistent, and real

OR

Just a fake like Jake, nothing to do, pretenders alley can't
validate that smile you reflect on that wall you call a face

Do you speak the truth or tell lies, remember the first lie
is to yourself then to others

Do you do what's right or slide wrong along faking
trying to make it to the other side?

How believable are you?

Your daily walk

Your daily conversations

Your meditations

Your creditability

Your trust worthiness

Your friendship

Your companionship

Your love

Your hope

Your commitments

Your dedications

Your WORD that is your BOND

Every day, Every moment, Every second we exercise our
beliefs if we truly do believe!!!!!

How is your faith?

Your actions

Faith without actions is dead

Faith is things hoped for

The evidence of things not seen

Death and life is in the tongue

Speak positive

Speak life

Speak truth

Speak confidence

Speak health

Speak love

Speak encouragement

Speak the WORD

Yet...Yet

BE CAREFUL WHAT YOU SPEAK

FOR YAH/YHVH SPOKE EVERYTHING INTO EXISTANCE

AS THE WORLD WAS SPOKEN

MAN AND WOMAN WAS MADE WHOLE

Your walk

Your talk

Your life

Dictates who you are in and out of light, behind closed doors, in the open out doors

Q'viva "the CHOSEN" are set apart, peculiar, distinct, in all mannerisms, lifestyle of everyday life.

IT IS NOT a religion, no cult, no tradition or language, IT IS WRITTEN as a way of life......

LIVE, LAUGH, LOVE & BE HAPPY EVERYDAY !!!!!!!!

LIVE LIFE TO THE FULLEST

~ERASED~

Living In A Meat Market Meant For Consumer Intakes. Life Is A Mystery! Yet Man Tries To Unfold Its Gates. With A Technology That's Over-Rated And Out Of Control. The Mind Is A Terrible Thing To Waste; Yet We Disintegrated Its Cells Day By Day. Look Around And See The Devastation It's Created!

Living In A World That's Slowly Becoming Devastated. By Its Own Potential, We Have No Clue Of What We Can Do And The Outcome It Will Do!

Excluding, Exclaiming, Sadly Abbreviating The Moments engulfed By Minutes Turned To Seconds. Could It Be We Are Being Erased? At A Glance At A Twinkling Of An Eye Not Taking Into Account The Lie?

We As People Living In America: Take Too Much For Granted; Our Freedom, Freedom To Speak, Our Rights, The Right To Choose, Live, Succeed Or Deteriorate At Any Rate.

True Fact I Was Privileged To Hear......

Yes Our Ancestors Died For A <u>Great Cause!</u>

The Cause Was The R I G H T The Right The Privilege To Have A Right To Voice Your Opinion, A Right To Vote, A Right To Live Where You Choose Free Of Persecution, A Right To Get An Education

A Right To Become A Citizen, A Right To Be Self Sufficient Amongst Other Things, A Right To Be Not Only Considered But Equal At All Cost, Yes, Our Ancestors Died And Gave Up A Lot To Accomplish This Plot. But, Isn't It My Right Now?? To Have The Right To Choose Rather To Vote Or Note, The Right To Accept What Other Choose To Hand Me On This So Called Silver Platter, A Right To Voice My Agreement Or Disagreement Approval Or Disapproval Out Loud; My Choice, My voice, My Opinion, My Right Becomes Just That..... What My Ancestors Left Me, Handed Down To Me, Willed To ,E With Their Bloodshed, Tear Stained, Sweaty Engraved Lives And Tortured Hands. I Choose Not To Vote For A Democracy That Does Not Include Me.......

Cause That's My Right! I Choose Not To Vote For Bondage Behind A Degree, For Prejudice With A Smile To Entrap Those Who Refuse To See Or Choose Not To Accept The Real Plan That's Been Painted Behind A Disguise To Fool Those Educated Gools Who Think They Got It All And Are Wise!

I Choose Not To Vote Or Accept The Education And History That Only Speaks Of Its Self Or Its Minor Views Of Us That Only Partially Include Or Is It Excludes A Story Of Any People Whose Been Tossed, Turned, Thrown, Humiliated And Torn A Division Left To Be Ignored If Possible Reborn. Are We Being Erased? A Part Of Us Have Those Who Identities Have Been Wiped From Their Memories And They Cannot Trace Their Ancestry, Lineage, History No Further

Than The United States Of America From Which They Did Not Begin Or Come But Forced To Accept Beyond Conditions Of Our Own To The Point We Now Accept A Lie Rather Than The Truth Of Who We Really Are!

Since It Is My Right To Choose What I Will And Will Not Accept Or Do,,, I Choose Not To Vote For Any Of You! Your Intentions Are Flawed, Fake, And Disgraceful You Close Your Eyes To Deceitfulness What You Have In Mind Is Simply Distasteful. "My People Are Destroyed For Lack Of Knowledge" Yochanan 1:1 - Handicapped By A Society They Did Not Choose. Left In A Land They Were Force Too, No Where To Go Have To Stay Where We Were Forced To Come Because We Know No More The Life Before Or How To Return To It So Now We Have To Learn To Live In Another World With Another People Who Are Harsher Than I Own. My People Are Blinded By Material Substance, Financial Gain Promises Not Kept And Greed Unexplained. When Its Easily Seen The Most High God Made Enough For All Of Us To Be. But Some Of Us You See Are To Selfishly Greedy Not Willing To Share Or Live Next To Where? No Unity Just Envy And Jealousy And Despair.

No Wonder Some People Can't Adjust, Can't Stand It Here! I'm Sure Our Ancestors Did Not Die For This Plight And I'm Sure They Would Turn Over A Trillion Times At The Sight Of What Is Occurring Here, How We Still Allow Being Misled In Fear By Not Becoming A Unit Here, Unlike Our Neighbors who Do It Well And Become Great Despite Adversity , Nostril Flare They Make A Stand Here! Yeah We Being Erased.......Little By Little Too Dumb

To Realize Our Fate!

Man Doesn't Realize His Estate, Man Only Knows That His Visions To Create Or

Procreate And His Dreams Demonstrate The Future He Intends To Incriminate By Creating Out Of His Mind Scientific Rate To Abolish Mankind A Human Race—A Species At Stake If Their Not Careful Will Be Over Taken!

Yes My People In particularly The Darker Hue Are Being Erased! Second By Second , Minute By Minute, Hour By Hour, Day By Day, Week By Week, Month By Month, Year By Year, Decade By Decade.... Can't You See How They Aare Trying To Vanish Our Lineage—Terminate Our Tribes, Creative Form Of Genocide. We Are Being Alienated & Eliminated ,Erased From

<u>His</u> / <u>Story</u>! At A Rate Undisclosed That Can't Be Denied By Mankind..

When It's Finally Realized It Will Be Too Late To Change The Line That Defines A Nation Cut Off This Time. **<u>Warnings</u>** We Fail To Adhere **<u>Alerts</u>** We Choose To Ignore **<u>Notices</u>** We Do Not Heed Anymore! Can You See We're Being Erased?

Silence Is Golden At Its' Appointed Time But, Have We Not Been Silent Enough. And At What Price Are We Willing To Lose This Time? His Story Will Always Repeat Itself Because It's His Story That Is Being Told That Must Evolve To A Greater Depth And

Truth Rising To The Occasion Of Self Worth If Not Death Is
Something We Use To Do, Should Do, Must Do And Do It Well!
Now Regardless of The Situation; Let's Not Stand Still And Be
Wiped Away, Tossed In An Effernol That's Washed Away......

ERASED!

NEVER HAD EXISTED.......

ERASED !

~WHERES THOU BEAUTY~

AMERICA THE BEAUTIFUL

I ASK

WHERE IS THY BEAUTY?

I FIND

SHE'S LOST IT, ERASED IT

NEVER HAD IT

FOR SHE'S FOUNDED UPON A BED OF LIES

CRIMINALITY, DISGRACE, DECEIT, PERSECUTION, DISEASE,
CORRUPTION AND DISTRUCTION....

WHERE IS THE BEAUTY IN THAT?

THERE IS NONE FOR IT NEVER WAS ESTABLISHED NOR DID
IT EVER EXIST......

YET WE PRAISE HER.....AMERICA

THE BEAUTIFUL WHERE DREAMS CAN COME TRUE

WHERE OPPORTUNITY EXISTS

WHERE FREEDOM DOES RING HIGH

AND

JUSTICE PREVAILS FOR THE VERY ELITE

THE BLIND LEAD THE BLIND

THE DEAF AND MUTE JUST SIT STILL

IT'S IRONIC THE POWER AMERICA HAS IF SHE'S NOT
CAREFUL SHE WILL FADE LIKE DEW UPON HER GRASS

AMERICA, AMERICA I ASK YOU AGAIN

WHERE IS THY BEAUTY?

IS IT HIDDEN WITHIN?

I SEEK OUT YOUR TERRAIN...

I ASK FOR MY SHARE

I KNOCK BUT YOU DON'T ANSWER

I FIND YOU IN DISPAIR AND NOT CLEAR

WHO'S WORTHY OF YOUR TREASURES

YOU'VE STOLEN FROM OTHERS HERE AND THERE?

WHERE IS THOU BEAUTY IN THAT?

~BIG MISTAKE~

America you made a BIG GIGANTIC MISTAKE when you took prayer out of schools, took parents' rights away, made discipline abuse, gave children the right to choose punishment...from what is written in the WORD of YHVH, divided church and state and government to not be holy and just..... according to the WORD.

What you have done is

You have given children the right to decide what is discipline is right in their eyes, made their schools a war ground, made the play grounds and parks a war zone, made the safety of the home an open diplomatic sewage not fit for a family.

You split the family up took the father out the home in order for the mother and children to survive then came back and made it where they both had to work to make a living making our kids the term used is latchkey kids left to defend for themselves. Made every day a work day no time for family ties or gatherings the blue laws made people take the time for family and children, husband and wife they did not have to choose like they do today.

You install daylight savings time when it really does not change the law of nature to make it any better we still need to turn lights on in the house we don't stay outside any longer it doesn't really help the seasons and nature changes without your help ...you just think you're doing something and you're not

You say it is unconstitutional to put a killer/murder in jail for life because he or she is underage where is it written you have the right to take a life and let the tax payers take care of them for the rest of their life like the victims' family are taking care of the murder/killer of their love one like Charles Mansfield yet states put people in prison for punishment that does not fit the crime Ludacris ....there was a time you make them serve the front lines in war if they made it back the sins were forgiven and they had paid their debt to society..... if they ran across enemy lines to survive they couldn't trade no secrets because they did not know any and they would

become traders left in a land to survive much different from which they came ...lets' get technical put a chip in them, their rights have been taken away anyway....when Europe got tired of its tyrants and taking care of crimes against humanity they excommunicated them from the land set them sail on the seas where they were suppose to die but YAH said differently.

You impose laws and punishments that don't fit the crime.....you crate right to work states where there's no accountability for those being fired. One thing is very noticeable when some companies had a monopoly on a service it was reasonable to have and maintain now with all the choices in the same enterprise the taxes and sub taxes and fees and charges it's amazing anyone can afford anything for a length of time.. YOU make changes supposedly for the better..... the question is?????
Better for WHO? Definitely not for those in the employed and unemployed class

How did the governments acquire Americas land they certainly did not buy it if they did we would not have reservations full of native American tribes, Hispanics would not have been ran out of California; Rosewood would not have been burn down and black wall street would still exist. If it was not for the incompetent of our own people and other people brought to the Americas it is for sure today would have been more satisfying maybe we all would have had a "Leave it to Beaver" scenario if it was not for the selfishness, jealousy, envy, greed, hatred for no reason, and the need to be in control of everything instead of lying, deceiving, and thriving upon the innocent, taking kindness for weakness, preying upon the passive those are Hellenistic ways even doing this today. You make it what it is instead of making it better than it was..

Try to make a difference start with the rich and famous who have more than they can possibly use they can find 5-10 families and put them in a home or give them ¼ acre of land to build on .... Pay off the deficient so America will be out of debt. America quit paying these other countries so much money if our factories are overseas that's funds going out two ways. INVEST in America bring America to the fore front once again. The rent should not be so high and cars should not cost 20 times the amount it took to produce the sale price is extremely high. There are so many things we can do to put money back in America instead of putting money overseas use good politics instead of the bad politics we are using. Our leaders make too much money and have too many accommodations at their leisure let's make America whole & fair again.

F Y I

The Americas was named after a Italian explorer by the
name of Amerigo Vespucci

In his honor

In

1557

~The Authors Digest~

Born and raised in Colorado

Scripting since the age of seven

Educated in Colorado, California, Washington, Georgia.

Has 1 brother and 2 sisters

Multi-talented

Birthed five gifts, adopted one gift Gifted twenty-two plus.

Single, divorced, engaged & widowed all in one breath

Many published works and

seven books

Accomplished various degrees, diplomas, and certifications

Awards, recognitions and scholarships.

Alumnus in many organizations and clubs

A believer and doer of the WORD

Spoken word artist

Composer of music and lyrics

Lover of poetry, drama, art

Lover if nature and chai

Reading is a pass time

Writing is a release

Meditating is a relaxation

Singing is a peace

Dancing is a freedom

Loving is a gift

I put my trust in YAH

ALL others I examined

My loyalty is in I AM

No other understands

It takes a village to raise a child

Done alone you have a mishap

Create in me a spirit of love

None greater than that above

Create in me the wisdom I need

To flourish like a seed

Create in me the patience

To glide the winds I breathe

Reachable

NJB Daniel-Dyer

c/o CSC

cnsbc_inc2003@yahoo.com

404.989.2072

Orders

Cited material & illustrations & Pictures

The Naming of America
http://www.uhmc.sunysb.edu/surgery/america.html

Amerigo Vespucci
http://library.thinkquest.org/4034/vespucci.html

WEB PICTURES

www.phibetaiota.net

letters from midlife . blog spot / America the beautiful

In America We Can Build On Dreams And Vision Of
Things Yet To Come

America Has Forgotten What It Was Built On When It
Began On Someone Elses Soil

The Lies And Fear From Which Its' Pilgrims Came
Fleeing Another Country To Start Over Again.

Pay Your Dues For The Wrongs You've Done

So The Blessings Will Come

PO-LI-TIK-N